Leveling Books K–6
Matching Readers to Text

Brenda M. Weaver

Skaneateles Central Schools

Skaneateles, New York, USA

INTERNATIONAL
Reading
Association

800 Barksdale Road, PO Box 8139
Newark, Delaware 19714-8139, USA
www.reading.org

Director of Publications   Joan M. Irwin
Assistant Director of Publications   Jeanette K. Moss
Editor in Chief, Books   Matthew W. Baker
Permissions Editor   Janet S. Parrack
Associate Editor   Tori Mello
Assistant Editor   Sarah Rutigliano
Publications Coordinator   Beth Doughty
Association Editor   David K. Roberts
Production Department Manager   Iona Sauscermen
Art Director   Boni Nash
Senior Electronic Publishing Specialist   Anette Schütz-Ruff
Electronic Publishing Specialist   Cheryl J. Strum
Electronic Publishing Assistant   Jeanine K. McGann

Project Editor   Janet Parrack

Library of Congress Cataloging in Publication Data
Weaver, Brenda M.
Leveling books K–6: matching readers to text/Brenda M. Weaver.
p.   cm.
Includes bibliographical references (p.) and index.
ISBN 0-87207-267-3 (alk. paper)
1. Reading (Elementary)   2. Book leveling.   3. Children—Books and reading.   I. Title
LB1573.W39   2000   00-024182

Dedicated to my supportive, loving Mom
and in memory of my Dad.

Contents

Introduction

Instruction in reading and writing has dramatically changed over the past 10 to 15 years. Traditionally, the teacher's predominant resource was the basal reader, but over the years, teachers shifted from the use of basals to literature or trade books. With this shift came numerous difficulties including the question of how to match books to students' reading levels. The terms *level* and *leveling* books are often confusing and misunderstood. For the purposes of this book, *level* or *leveling* means to analyze the text in order to match the text to the reader based on the reader's competencies.

The traditional basal reader had a preplanned selection order for each student, and teachers generally followed this plan. Because basals used controlled vocabularies in their stories, the level of a book or its readability was easily determined. The traditional basal followed a leveling system, or structure of how books are presented to students, of preprimer, primer, 1-2, 2-1, 2-2, 3-1, 3-2, 4, 5, and 6. These levels were determined by the number of words or syllables in a sentence and the number of sentences in a text passage, as well as by the selection of skills to be used in instruction or scope and sequence of skills. The levels were mostly consistent from series to series, and instruction focused primarily on students acquiring reading skills based on the learning theory of that time.

The education picture changed as research revealed more about how learning takes place and that learning is more complex and multifaceted than once believed. To be successful in learning, students need to have meaningful experiences, build on their previous knowledge, learn and apply strategies, receive feedback, and have a positive climate in which to learn (Brandt, 1998). These new aspects of learning required changes in and new instructional techniques and activities and, thus, required a change in how books are used in instruction.

Developing an appropriate leveling system and selection criteria for books so that students experience gradual challenges in their reading and become successful readers and writers became a challenge for many teachers.

Several educators provide guidance on selecting and leveling based on the most recently understood aspects of learning. Routman (1988) provides lists of books to use at the different levels of reading instruction and lists them according to what teachers have found successful. Mooney (1988) describes the essential characteristics for books at the emergent, early, and fluency levels of reading. Mooney also was instrumental in developing core books used in the New Zealand national curriculum and those distributed in the United States as the Ready to Read program. In *Guided Reading: Good First Teaching for All Children,* Fountas and Pinnell (1996) discuss the characteristics of the text levels, the observable behaviors at these levels, and provide extensive book lists for each level. The authors ask for feedback on their levels since readability gaps may exist between levels. Fountas and Pinnell take the process a step further in *Matching Books to Readers: Using Leveled Books in Guided Reading, K–3* (1999) in which more books are listed and the levels are defined more clearly. Cooper (1993) explains and describes four basic criteria for the selection of books: developmental appropriateness, student appeal, literary quality, and cultural and social authenticity. Clay (1991) discusses text choice and text supports, which allow students easier access to the text and makes it easier to read. Text supports include books that are predictable, repetitive, and close to a student's natural language.

Clay (1991) also presents several approaches to examining the gradient difficulty of texts, including using a publishing company's system or devising a system based on students' learning responses in a school or district. Clay cautions, however that any system regardless of origin will not be appropriate for all children. Therefore, teachers must make informed decisions about which books and which leveling system to use in instruction.

The intent of *Leveling Books K–6* is to assist teachers in making those decisions. This book discusses the need for leveling books, the critical understandings that influence leveling, the steps to leveling, and some comparisons of leveling systems in use with these new instructional techniques or this process approach. Chapter 1 explains why leveling books has become many educators' greatest need when using new instructional techniques. Chapter 2 explains the many aspects of the new instructional techniques for the process approach to reading and writing. Knowledge and understanding of these aspects influence how teachers select books, level books, evaluate students, and deliver instruction.

Chapter 3 provides a step-by-step procedure for leveling books in grades K–6. These generic procedures become specific once a teacher selects a leveling system to use in the classroom. Several leveling systems are available to teachers, and careful selection is important, since all instruction focuses on the books selected. Chapter 4 reviews some of the more widely used leveling systems using specific criteria. Chapter 5 presents a detailed description of my own leveling system, which has been used successfully for 12 years. It is compared to other systems in Chapter 4, using the same criteria. Chapter 6 provides suggestions for beginning the task of leveling books.

Teachers want to learn and use all the necessary strategies and skills in order for their students to become successful readers and writers. This book will help guide teachers through the important process of how to level books and will help both administrators and teachers find ways to customize their own literature-based programs to fit the specific needs of their students.

Chapter 1

The Need for Leveling Books

Jason's first-grade teacher referred him to me because he was experiencing difficulty in learning to read. She wanted another opinion on how she might help him be more successful.

I took him to the reading room for a diagnostic teaching activity. "How are you doing in reading, Jason?" I asked as we walked down the hall. "Oh, I love reading. I like to read the dinosaur books," said Jason. "That's exciting. Let me see if I can find a dinosaur book you can read to me today. I want to see how you read," I responded. Jason smiled. "I hope you can find one on T Rex," replied Jason.

A few hours later, I went to another first-grade teacher to assess Karen, a new student who had moved from another district. She needed to be tested on our benchmarks to determine the appropriate level for instruction. I asked Karen where she was from and how she liked reading. She responded, "I can't read. I just look at the pictures. I don't know the sounds." After testing her, I found she was at the same benchmark level for instruction as Jason.

(Brenda M. Weaver, fall 1997, Skaneateles Central Schools, Skaneateles, New York)

This vignette depicts the most essential needs teachers have for leveling books: to motivate children to read, to provide them with successful reading experiences, and to identify reading difficulties early enough to provide intervention instead of remediation. Jason's reading experiences had been successful. He had been provided with books appropriate for his level of reading ability. His difficulty was that he had not made the expected progress through the levels, therefore, other techniques were necessary. On the other hand, Karen's reading experiences in first grade had not been successful, and, therefore, she thought she could not read.

Before leveled books were used in our district, Karen's attitude was the norm, and students with Jason's difficulties went unnoticed for several months or until a standardized test was given. However, the use of leveled books has provided teachers with knowledge that students are experiencing difficulty that requires attention. Previously, students like Jason might not have received extra help until they had failed.

A Look Back

In the past, teachers used basals with a set difficulty progression. However, the basal levels were based on different reading and learning research and on text that was controlled for words and contrived as it developed.

The basal readers of the 1960s through the early 1980s were based on the research and theory that children first needed to learn skills and words before they could read with fluency and understanding or comprehension. However, although students were able to read the words fluently, they often did not comprehend what they read nor could they apply their developing knowledge to reading "real books." The emphasis on decoding skills did not automatically foster comprehension (Cooper, 1993). To help counteract this situation, programs included the study of comprehension skills such as main idea, sequencing, and drawing conclusions, but teaching these skills in isolation did not remedy the situation. Through the research efforts of many including Vygotsky (1978) and Clay (1979), educators began to realize that reading is more complex and involves other aspects in order to acquire meaning from print. However, educators remained consistent in their view that we teach reading to assist students in acquiring meaning from print.

Cooper (1993) explains that students need to construct their own meaning as they read. They need to learn various strategies such as how to decode an unfamiliar word in text, set their purpose for reading, and apply their knowledge of text type as they read. Reading literature provides the meaningful context in which students can develop these strategies. But because of the range of readability levels in literature books, teachers need to provide a systematic way to present the literature.

Leveling Systems

For the purposes of this book, a *leveling system* is defined as the structure used to sequence the books used in a literacy program in a classroom or school. A system generally consists of a defined framework, instructional activities and techniques using leveled books, and assessments. It is what and how teachers instruct in their classrooms and how it is evaluated and reported. Leveling books is selecting text to match the competencies of a reader or writer using a leveling system. However, some leveling systems are limited and do not successfully and efficiently fulfill these needs.

Therefore, teachers need to choose leveling systems that match both their goals of instruction and their students' needs.

Teacher Needs

Most teachers identify two fundamental needs for leveling books: providing literacy instruction that fits the needs of their students and finding methods to select materials. Previously, basal readers provided for these needs. Teachers followed the basals' sequence, and the materials were readily available.

Two things changed this convenient and comfortable use of basal systems. First, more advanced understandings about learning were identified by research (Brandt, 1998). Brandt summarizes these important understandings: People learn through meaningful experiences by constructing new knowledge from present knowledge, by socially interacting, and by accepting challenging but achievable goals. People learn differently, need feedback, and function better with a positive emotional climate. Other important understandings include that learning is developmental, involves the use of strategies, and is influenced by environment. Therefore, we know that more effective learning takes place when all these understandings are present in literacy development.

Second, many basals are constructed using selections from literature that may or may not contain the appropriate skills at a given level. These basals appear to base their selections on child interest rather than how closely the text will support instruction in a specific area. In the past, the scope and sequence and the levels for a basal defined the progression of student learning, which is no longer the case. Now, with the process approach to literacy development and current understandings of literacy, books and basal readers are selected based on the competencies and needs of students. The teachers' responsibility is to identify the competencies of their students and match these competencies to texts that are supportive and challenging. For these reasons, teachers seek leveling systems that provide for these needs.

Student Needs

In order to provide appropriate instruction teachers need to identify the strengths and weaknesses of their students. A leveling system that includes assessment will help serve this need. To be successful, students need a well-rounded, well-balanced literacy program, one that fits their individual needs as well as the standards of the state or nation.

Moreover, students require a balanced approach to instruction using literature. For example, they need experience with various genre, a variety of content, and different types of books. In order to provide this, teachers have to be well rounded in their use of literature in instruction.

Although using literature for reading instruction is seen as positive, there can be disadvantages. As students progress from grade to grade, the use of different leveling systems at each grade can cause students to experience difficulties. The expectations and assessments for different leveling systems can vary and thereby result in student frustration or discouragement. In order to avoid this situation within a school, teachers are encouraged to select the same leveling system. It is even more beneficial if the same leveling system is used district-wide. Having one leveling system will provide consistency and ensure continued progress for students.

Curriculum Needs

During the last decade, teachers and curriculum developers have witnessed a shift from traditional content-based curriculum to those with a strategy or process approach. This shift along with curriculum innovations such as cooperative learning, whole language, and critical thinking skills has encouraged teachers and school administrators to revise their curriculums to incorporate these changes. Moreover, striving to identify and raise standards at both the state and national levels has put pressure on educators to refine and realign their curriculum to meet these new standards. Although the literature supports the shift to a process-based curriculum (Nolan & Francis, 1992; Brandt, 1988; Presseisen, 1988; Fullan, 1991), administrators and teachers struggle to incorporate this approach and new standards in their curriculums. School administrators and teachers seek leveling systems that will help them write their curriculums and incorporate these changes.

Additional curriculum needs include providing consistent instruction and equal access to education for all students. In order for instruction to be consistent across grade levels and within a school district, the selection and use of texts must support a teacher's own program as well as the school and district curriculum. Teachers' programs and school programs also must be congruent with what recent research says about literacy development. As educators we need to include all students in our programs regardless of their needs. Leveling systems can address these needs and provide the structure for consistent instruction and curriculum scope and sequences.

Chapter 2

Understanding the Dynamics of Book Leveling

When we started using literature, the teachers were confused about using it in their classrooms. They knew the children were very motivated with the literature stories, but which skills and strategies should they instruct with each book? How should they teach them and when? The Weaver Framework provided the what, when, and how that we were looking for in using literature. It made all the difference in the world in creating a literature-based program. Our standardized test scores demonstrated the results: up from 66% passing to 94% passing. The children are getting wonderful literature along with skills and strategies in their classrooms. They are successful readers and writers.

(Lois Weinstein, reading teacher, Liberty Central Schools, Liberty, New York)

Teachers are discovering that there are key elements to providing their students with a successful literacy program: framework, assessment, and instruction. English (1986) supports this and asserts that unless a program includes these three elements, it may not be successful. He also stresses that these elements must be closely integrated. The framework provides the structure for the expectations and content of literacy, that is, the scope and sequence of skills and strategies. The instruction provides the activities and the opportunity for students to learn the skills and strategies, while practicing with books. The assessment is presented in the same manner as the instruction and assesses the framework. This close bond is essential for an effective program. The three elements are the basis for any leveling system. In a specific leveling system, how the books are leveled is partially influenced by their use in instruction. The instructional focus is influenced by the developed framework with the assessment being used to evaluate both instruction and the framework.

Teachers realize the importance of understanding the reading-writing process, the elementary aspects of genre study, and the appropriate student expectations for instruction. This knowledge influences a teacher's decision in the selection of leveled books for instruction. Teachers know that using the appropriate book can make the difference between opening a new world for a student or causing frustration and lack of motivation in reading. The following discussion looks at these elements and understandings more closely.

Framework

The framework provides the structure or focus for literacy instruction. It helps teachers focus, plan, and deliver their instruction.

The framework for leveling can be selected or developed. The purpose of a framework is to shape the objectives and aspects of instruction. The leveled books, which match these frameworks, support the instruction and are used in the assessments. For example, the primary objective in Reading Recovery (see page 40) is to develop oral fluency. The leveled books are sequenced based on the challenges of the text structure. In the running records, the books used are examples of the text difficulty for that level based on how easy or difficult they are to read. Identifying the purposes for which you select a framework or developing one on your own is vital to the success of your literacy program.

The framework needs to reflect other aspects as well. A framework should be selected that supports local, state, or national standards. The framework should incorporate or expand what you already do in literacy instruction. Most importantly, it must fulfill the teacher's needs or those of the school.

If the purpose of a framework is to provide a program for several grade levels, then you need to select or develop one that creates a balance in your instruction and assessment. For example, if a framework is to serve K–6 literacy development, then it must provide for a variety of genres to be used and assessed over the grade levels. A large inclusive framework takes into account all these aspects of instruction and provides the structure for the program and the leveling system.

Assessment

When we first used levels in our literacy program, assessment tools were mainly observational and not specifically defined. Teachers were unsure when children had achieved the appropriate skills and strategies, and consequently had difficulty knowing when to move them to the next level. Therefore, some children remained at a level for 10 to 15 weeks, while others moved to the next level in 4 to 6 weeks. When teachers were questioned about the children's movement to other levels, it was clear that teachers had set their own expectations and made individual interpretations of the assessment aspects. Therefore, it was difficult to build consensus because the assessment was subjective. But, once the assessment was changed and more clearly defined in terms of performance behaviors, the children's competencies became more similar at each level, and they easily progressed from level to level.

Assessment is a vital element to a leveling system, because the task requirements of the assessments shape and drive the instruction. As teachers, we want the evaluation of our job performance to be based on our responsibilities. The same is true with the instruction and assessment of children. We want to closely match what we are teaching with what we are assessing. When the two are not congruent, the assessment is inadequate. Often, teachers find this problem when standardized tests are used to evaluate reading, and the test's task is to match the sounds in words: Matching sounds in words is difficult to equate with the actual reading of text.

We want to match the assessment to the framework and reflect what we want students to know and do. A balance between skills and strategies is necessary also in order to reflect the current research in how children learn. For example, we know that using the meaning strategy as well as phonics instruction is vital in learning to read. The question is not about which to use, but rather how to balance the skills and strategies for effective learning to take place. Assessment should incorporate this concept as well. If only skills are assessed, vital strategies may be lost, and the converse is true. Assessments need to reflect both skills and strategies in order to provide children with a balanced approach to learning to read and write, as well as learning from reading and writing.

Lastly, assessment must include what you already do and how you expand or revise these aspects to provide a clearly defined assessment tool that is effective in assessing what children are learning and identifying what needs to be retaught for those children who are less competent.

Instruction

The first step in selecting a leveling system is to develop or select the framework with the appropriate assessment for your needs. The next step is to use this framework to provide instruction using leveled books that support the instruction by giving children practice in specific areas at their own level. The teacher's lesson plans reflect the aspects of the framework for those leveled books. The assessments help the teacher to identify at which level in the leveling system the student should be placed. In preparing the lessons, the teacher selects a book at the student's level and plans the instruction.

These books then can be used in different types of reading: *shared reading, guided reading*, and *independent reading*. *Shared reading* is the whole-group or class reading of a text. The books are usually selected so the majority of students can be successful with them. Shared reading is oral reading at kindergarten and Grade 1, and silent reading at grades 2–6. All students in the class will require the same book for instruction. *Guided reading* involves instruction with small groups of students. The groups are formed using students' ability levels, skill needs, genre or title. For shared and guided reading, the teacher creates instructional plans. For *independent reading*, students select their own books to read silently. With children (K–2), it is better to preselect books, place them in boxes according to levels, and have children select their books from the appropriate boxes. Students in third grade and higher seem to make more appropriate level choices for independent reading.

Matching the Weaver Reading/Writing Stages With Framework, Assessment, and Instruction

This leveling system and literacy program integrates reading and writing beginning in kindergarten. (See Chapter 5 for a more detailed description.) The following examples show the close relationship between framework, assessment, and instruction. The first example is for primary students and the second is for intermediate students. Leveling systems in the primary grades will focus on developing reading fluency, using literal comprehension skills and strategies. Leveling systems in the intermediate grades will focus on learning vocabulary and content from the text, developing an understanding of author styles, and genre.

Example 1: Beginning Grade 1

RW 4 Focus Aspects
Oral Reading

1. Understands how reading goes when there is more than one line of print (left to right and return).
2. Uses picture cues and initial sounds to pronounce unknown words.
3. Orally explains book read.
4. Reads text with 90% accuracy rate.

Other Conventions of Print/Skills

1. Follows words in text while story is being read and recognizes when words or sentences are out of sequence.
2. Isolates one and two letters in print.

3. Identifies first and last letter of a word in book.

4. Identifies and explains use of comma and quotation marks.

5. Identifies the consonant sounds at the beginning and ending of words.

Writing

1. Writes a simple sentence using initial and final consonants.

The following teacher directions for the assessment at RW 4 are from the *Weaver Reading/Writing Stages: Benchmark Assessment Guide*, using *Green Footprints* (1989) by Connie Kehoe. (This assesment is an example and not intended for use out of context.) The directions demonstrate that both skills and strategies are assessed and clearly define the criteria of competency in a format which reflects performance behaviors.

Reading/Writing Stage 4—Teacher Directions

Oral Reading (Individual)

1. Distribute the book. Ask the child to point to the title of the book. The teacher reads the title as the child points to the words. The teacher and child discuss the cover and title and what it might be about.

2. Have the child walk through the story using the pictures. Child talks about where the footprints are going. Teacher does not specifically give input except with the baby doll distinction.

3. Ask child to point to where he should begin to read. Have child read book and point to the words as he reads. Teacher takes oral reading record by writing down the errors made on the Oral Reading Record Form. For example: "look/like" means the child said "look" for the word *like*. It is suggested that a check or slash be used to indicate a correct reading of a word. Reminder: Oral reading errors are mispronunciations, substitutions, omissions, and teacher pronounced words.

4. Ask the child to tell what the book was about. Teacher dates the items in oral reading for which the criterion is met.

Other (Individual with book)

1. Teacher has child return to pages 6 and 7. Teacher asks child to point to sentences as teacher reads and decide what is wrong with the teacher's reading. Teacher says: Green footprints run across the floor. (Child explains what

is wrong with the teacher's reading.) Green footprints out the house. (Child explains what is wrong with the teacher's reading.)

2. Teacher asks child to point to one letter, two letters, first letter in a word, and last letter in a word.

3. Take Item 8 worksheet and distribute to student. Read sentence to child as he points. Ask child to point to comma and explain purpose. Ask child to point to quotation marks and explain purpose.

Other (Group)

1. Present worksheet on consonants and say words for child to circle letters. Initial: (ball, foot, mother, sat, roof, pat, run, down, wet, note, house, lamb, kite, cabbage, garage, vet, you, jump, zoo)
   Final: (bib, roof, dim, hill, hit, sip, car, load, hike, torn)

Writing (Group)

1. Ask child to draw a picture of something he saw that made footprints. Ask child to write at least one sentence about it.

After the assessment has been given, the Rubric Decision-Making Scoring Chart (see below) can be used to determine the placement of the student. Students who have met the criteria for RW 4 will move to RW 5 as indicated on the chart. Those students not successful with stage RW 4 will either remain for additional instruction or move to the next level as a RW 5 SP for reteaching in the RW 4 and an introduction to RW 5. The placement levels are dependent on the criteria met.

RW 4 Rubric Decision-Making Scoring Chart		
Continue to Teach at RW 4	**Transition to RW 5 Sp**	**Teach at RW 5**
Unable to meet criterion for item RW 4 D or missed 3 or more items.	Passed RW 4 D, RW 4 I, and did not miss more than 2 items.	Passed all items.
Note: If students fall between categories, the teacher must judge whether they should move ahead or remain at level for further instruction.		

Using the skills and strategies from the framework and assessment, the instruction will follow similar guidelines with books that support this instruction. At the RW 4 Stage, the children will read books to practice the picture cue strategy and begin to use initial sounds to assist with unfamiliar words. Therefore, the text needs to be somewhat repetitive, with pictures supporting the text but with decodable words that can be practiced by applying initial sounds. The text needs to have two to three lines of print so children can practice reading left to right and returning to the left. The book should contain simple sentences with many high-frequency or sight-vocabulary words. An example of this type of book is *Animals* (1997) by Paul Reeder.

The instruction used with this text is similar to the assessment guidelines. Have the students read the text and practice all the aspects to be assessed. The teacher provides instruction in initial and final consonant sounds, various conventions of print, and writing. The following is a typical 5-day instructional guide:

Day 1: Teacher and students look through text and predict what book is about. Students orally read text and teacher assists them in applying picture cues, meaning cues, and initial sound cues.

Day 2: Students reread text for fluency and identify differences between letters and words. Teacher presents sentence strips containing quotes from text. Students identify quotation marks and commas.

Day 3: On chart paper, teacher lists animals mentioned in text. Teacher and students discuss the initial sounds of these words. Students generate other words that begin with the same sound and write them beneath each animal's name. Students practice identifying and stating the initial and final sounds of objects in pictures. Teacher can also use letters and word families to practice reading words using initial sounds.

Day 4: Teacher distributes sentence strips from text. Students practice reading the strips without the use of picture cues. If necessary, students can use the text to check their reading. Students reread the text.

Day 5: Students select an animal from the text or another that they like. They draw a picture and write sentences describing their animal. Teacher assists with spelling in the editing stage after students finish writing. These pages can be made into a book for the students to share.

When the students can easily perform these tasks, they can be assessed and moved up a level (see chart on page 13). Matching the framework, assessment, and instruction provides for effective, efficient learning and provides the teacher with an opportunity to instruct diagnostically. The teacher can observe those students who have difficulty with oral fluency or learning sounds and then provide additional instruction in those areas.

The following framework example provides instruction in comparing and contrasting narrative and expository writing, which are important skills and strategies for upper elementary students as they enter the middle school level.

Example 2: Beginning Grade 5

Necessary Elements/Strategies for 5.1
Key: LB = *The Language Book* (1991)   WS = *Write Source 2000* (1995)

Reading

1. Define narration and exposition (WS, 127).
2. Differentiate between narrative/expository text (WS, 078).
3. Identify and discuss story elements (WS, 387).
4. Identify and discuss point of view (LB, 187;WS, 387).

Writing

1. Understand expository writing (LB, 169–170, 225).
2. Understand narrative writing (LB, 123, 165–166, 185–190, 227).
3. Understand characteristics of different genres (see end papers of *The Language Book*).
4. Write to meet both the specific form and topic.

Review and Expansion Elements/Strategies for 5.1.

Reading

1. Utilize skimming and scanning (LB, 205–206).
2. Utilize paraphrasing (LB, 210).

Writing

1. Understand report-writing process (LB, 202–204).
2. Understand story writing (LB, 123–124, 185–190).

Assessment tasks on narrative and expository writing for 5.1.

Reading

Student is presented with two pieces of writing to read.

1. In a paragraph, identify which piece is expository and which is narrative. Support your choices with reasons.

2. Write a brief summary of the narrative piece.

3. List four (4) facts from the expository piece.

4. At the end of the story, the three men felt that the jewels in their pockets were not as valuable as the real jewels of axolotyl. What did the author mean by his statement? Explain by using details from the story.

5. Both pieces discuss how working cooperatively can be valuable. Explain how this statement is true for both pieces. Use details from both pieces to support your answer.

Writing

1. Select one topic:
school
a specific sport
an out-of-school activity

2. Write two separate paragraphs on the same topic: one narrative and one expository.

In the following example, the teacher uses the book *The Bridge to Terabithia* (1977) by Katherine Paterson. Because this novel will take several weeks to complete, it will be necessary for the teacher to include both expository and narrative understandings. The following is a typical 5-week instructional guide, which incorporates both the framework or instructional focus and the assessments.

Week 1: Instruct in the elements of narrative text. Read the first two chapters and have students identify these elements. Have students complete a reading guide with one or two questions for each chapter as they read. These questions focus on higher level thinking skills such as author's message or interpretation of meaning.

Week 2: Instruct in elements of expository text. Use a student magazine article or a content subject textbook such as a science textbook and have students identify the expository elements. Instruct in the understanding of fact versus opinion. Have students identify the facts and opinions (if present) in the expository text. Have them read two more chapters in *The Bridge to Terabithia* and complete the guide questions.

Week 3: Have students read three more chapters and complete the guide questions. Also ask students to write a fictional account of an incident that happened at school. Remind them to include the elements of narrative. This writing should be no longer than two pages. After completing their writings, have the students share them while the other students write a list of the narrative elements present in each piece such as the characters or the problem. The writers of the pieces can use the feedback to revise their pieces.

Week 4: Have students read three more chapters and answer the guide questions. After completing this task, ask them to write an expository piece (a couple of paragraphs) that describes an animal or insect that could have been found in Jess and Leslie's special place. Students and teacher will review pieces for expository elements.

Week 5: Have students read the remaining chapters and answer the guide questions. Ask students to write a personal response to the text.

The close relationship of framework, assessment, and instruction determines the success of the system in developing literacy. The correlation of these three elements will provide consistent, efficient instruction and promote students' continuous progress through the levels. Students can be assessed for any difficulties and provided with intervention strategies to address them quickly.

Nature of Reading and Writing

In addition to the key elements of the leveling system, a teacher's knowledge of the reading and writing process is necessary so that in looking at a text he or she can decide if it is highly supportive to a reader at a specific level. In this process approach, Cooper (1993) identifies four principles that will guide the construction of meaning in reading:

1. Learners develop reading, writing, listening, speaking, and thinking simultaneously.
2. Learners learn to read and write by actually reading, writing, and responding to their reading and writing.
3. Learners' prior knowledge and background are key elements in their ability to construct meaning.
4. Comprehension is the process of constructing meaning by relating ideas from the text to the learner's prior knowledge and background.

The instructional focus of the reading and writing process shifts as the learner develops reading and writing skills. In the primary grades the focus areas include print conventions, cueing strategies/word study, comprehension and response/writing. The intermediate grades focus on word study, comprehension/study skills, genre specifics, and response/writing. Figures 1 and 2 (see pages 18 and 19) give specific details about which skills and strategies to focus on and the progression of development that can be expected in each area.

As you begin to understand the process approach to reading and writing, you will be better able to identify the leveling system needed in your classroom and how to instruct using leveled books.

Figure 1: Aspects of Reading and Writing, K to Mid-Grade 3

Learning to Read and Write

Print Conventions

Location of print.
Identification of cover/title.
Left to right reading.
Identification of words in text.
Identification of letters in words.
Knowledge of capital and small letters.
Understanding of period.
Understanding of question mark.
Understanding of exclamation point.
Understanding of comma.
Understanding of other punctuation (i.e., quotations) and text formats (i.e., bold, italic).
Knowledge of sentence concept.

Comprehension

Use of picture.
Use of text.
Retell text.
Summarize text.
Knowledge of literary elements:
  title, author, setting,
  characters, summary of plot,
  climax, problem/resolution.
Understanding of comprehension patterns.
Understanding of text organization.
Understanding of genres.
Use of study skills.

Cueing Strategies/Word Study

Meaning of pictures.
Voice/print match.
Word/syllable segmentation.
Distinguish word detail.
Use of language structure.
Use of self-correction.
Meaning of text.
Application of initial & final sounds.
Sound segmentation.
Application of medial sounds.
Application of sight vocabulary.
Integration of all strategies/skills.
Understanding of prefixes, suffixes, roots.
Learns vocabulary from text reading.

Response/Writing

Orally relates picture & text.
Orally retells.
Orally summarizes.
Draws pictures to respond.
Uses experience in response.
Writes random letters/words.
Writes inventive words.
Writes inventive and conventional words.
Writes conventional words.
Writes groups of words.
Writes sentences.
Use of mechanics of writing.
Writes for purpose.
Use of experience and text to respond.
Writes with style, organization, and appropriate format.

Figure 2: Aspects of Reading and Writing, Mid-Grade 3 Through Grade 6

Learning From Reading and Writing

Word Study

Application of all cueing strategies.

Develop reading vocabulary through the use of context and resources (i.e., dictionary).

Develop technical vocabulary (vocabulary specific to text content).

Understand the multiple meanings of words and how to use them.

Understand the origins of words and how to identify these origins in unfamiliar words.

Understand how to generate and use synonyms and antonyms of vocabulary words.

Understand how to explain the definitions of words to others.

Comprehension/Study Skills

Understanding the literal meaning of the text.

Understanding the interpretive meaning of the text.

Understanding of more advanced literary elements (i.e., theme, tone, mood, and symbolism).

Understanding of comprehension patterns and how they convey the author's message.

Understanding of text organization and format for author's purpose.

Understanding of resource aids such as index, glossary.

Understanding how to use own experiences and text to apply knowledge in another context.

Develops note taking skills.

Genre Specifics

Identify features of genre.

Understand the features of genre.

Identify comprehension pattern(s) used in genre and how it helps to convey message.

Identify and understand the study skills necessary to comprehend genre piece.

Understand how the features of the genre used promote the message of the author.

Response/Writing

Understands that written response involves use of text and own experiences.

Writes responses which reflect text and own experiences.

Writes using a variety of sentence structures to convey meaning.

Writes with appropriate punctuation, capitalization, grammar, and spelling.

Writes with appropriate style, organization, and format for a specific purpose or intent.

Writes using vivid, interesting language which motivates the reader to visualize.

Grade-Level Expectations

The chart of grade-level expectations (see Figure 3 on pages 20–21) was developed using my experiences with children as well as recent research and is meant as a guideline for curriculum development. The expectations are developed with an

Figure 3: Grade-Level Expectations

Grade Level	Print Conventions	Word Study	Comprehension	Genre Specifics	Response/ Writing
K	Locates print. Reads left to right. Identifies period.	Meaning of pictures.	Uses pictures to understand.	Knows different types of books.	Orally relates picture and text. Orally retells Writes random letters.
1	Knows alphabet. Identifies words. Understands period, question mark, comma, exclamation point.	Voice/print match. Language segmentation. Distinguishes word detail. Uses initial sounds. Uses language structure.	Uses pictures to understand. Uses text. Retells text.	Some understanding of real and fantasy.	Orally relates picture and text. Orally retells Draws pictures to respond. Writes random letters and words. Writes inventive words.
2	Understands other punctuation. Understands sentence.	Uses self-correction. Applies sounds. Some learning of vocabulary from text reading.	Retells text Summarizes text. Knows some of literary elements.	Identifies fiction and non-fiction.	Writes inventive and conventional words. Writes simple sentences.
3		Learns vocabulary from text. Applies sounds. Understands affixes. Integrates cueing strategies.	Summarizes text. Knows literary elements. Understands some comprehension patterns. Understands literal and some interpretive text.	Identifies features of genres.	Predominant use of conventional words. Uses experience and text to respond. Uses mechanics in writing.

(continued)

Figure 3: Grade-Level Expectations *(continued)*

Grade Level	Print Conventions	Word Study	Comprehension	Genre Specifics	Response/ Writing
4		Applies reading strategies. Develops reading vocabulary from text.	Understands comprehension patterns. Understands literal and interpretive meaning of text. Uses study skills.	Understands features of genres. Understands some relationship of genre and message. Understands comprehension patterns and genre.	Uses mechanics consistently Writes for a purpose. Uses experience and text to respond.
5		Applies reading strategies. Develops reading vocabulary from text. Understands multiple meanings.	Understands advanced literary elements. Understands patterns and how relates to author's message. Uses study skills.	Understands relationship of genre and message. Uses study skills to understand genre.	Writes with style, organization, and appropriate format. Writes with a variety of sentence structures to convey message.
6		Understands origins of words. Explains definitions to others.	Uses resource aids. Uses text and experience to apply in another context. Develops note taking skills.	Understands how genre features promote message of author.	Writes with style, organization, and appropriate format for a specific purpose. Uses vivid language.

Figure 4: Guidelines to Genre

Genre	Grades for Instruction	Reading Assessment	Writing Assessment
Folktales	2, 3, 4, 5	3, 4	5
Myths	5, 6	6	6
Fables	3, 4, 5	4	5
Legends	4, 5, 6	5	6
Picture books	K–6 Read alouds	Depends on book	5
Epic literature	Read aloud		
Fantasy	3, 4, 5, 6	6	6
Science fiction	3, 4, 5, 6	5	6
Realistic fiction	2, 3, 4, 5, 6	4, 5, 6	6
Poetry:	see Types	4	6
Ballad	5–6		
Narrative	Read aloud		
Lyric	Read aloud		
Sonnet	Read aloud		
Free verse	Read aloud		
Limerick	5–6		
Haiku	3–4		
Cinquain	4–5		
Diamante	Read aloud		
Tanka	Read aloud		
Concrete	4–5		
Informational books	2, 3, 4, 5, 6	3, 4, 5, 6	3, 4, 5, 6
Historical fiction	4, 5, 6	5	6
Mystery	2, 3, 4, 5, 6	3	4
Drama	5, 6	5	Beyond 6
Biography	3, 4, 5, 6	4	5
Newspapers/ Magazines	4, 5, 6	5	6
Books of true experience	4, 5, 6	5	6
Essays, journals, letters, Personal accounts	5, 6	6	6
Historical documents/ Speeches	4, 5, 6	6	Beyond 6

average student at a particular grade level. These expectations are met by students of average ability by the end of that grade level. Please keep in mind that although all aspects are introduced and instructed, they may not be appropriate for completion until the designated grade; for example, "orally relates picture and text." Although kindergarten students are expected to be able to respond in this way, the technique is used in all grades.

Genre Study at the Elementary Level

The use and study of genre in the elementary grades is relatively recent. The whole language movement, which began in the late 1980s, emphasized the use of literature in the elementary classroom. Teachers became excited about using children's literature in their classrooms and more children's literature books were published. Teachers now have thousands of books to choose from for classroom instruction. Because authors use different genres to convey their messages, teachers must discuss and instruct genre for comprehension. However, some genres may be too difficult for elementary children to understand.

Figure 4 helps give teachers a sense of which genres to emphasize at which grade levels. It can be used for curriculum development but is intended more specifically for leveling books.

In terms of instruction, the grade levels listed only suggest when it is appropriate for teachers to use a particular genre in instruction and provide student reading materials of this genre. The reading and writing assessment columns suggest which grade levels can use in-depth study of the genre and subsequent assessments. Please note that writing in the genre and reading the genre may be different. Reading books of a specific genre to children is always encouraged regardless of the level. Children can appreciate and comprehend various genres at all grades.

This chapter presented the key elements and understandings that affect and influence the leveling of books. While assessing books for sentence structure and text support, you are also observing which text organization and genre are appropriate for the reader. Each of these elements and understandings influences which books to select for a child's reading instruction.

Chapter 3

Preparation and Steps for Leveling Books

Wow! I can't believe you have so many books in your book room. I like the way you have organized the levels using colors. Each title has an instructional guide. That's a lot of work. It makes me want to reorganize and level all the books in my classroom.

(Visitor Survey, October 1996, Waterman Elementary School, Skaneateles, New York)

Before you begin leveling your own books, you will need to make a few decisions. Which leveling system will you use? How will you label your books—by color or level number? Where will you store your books? In addition, you should know and understand the terms used in leveling books.

Understanding Leveling Terms

Text support is the focal point for determining the difficulty of text. In the leveling process, three areas help determine the amount of text support: format, language structure, and content. These three areas will influence whether a text is easy and has a lot of text support or is difficult and has minimal text support in order to match the text to a reader's competencies.

Format

Format is how the text looks and is organized, and format is influenced by the amount of print, size of print, print location and spacing, and print conventions such as punctuation and capitalization. The amount and size of print is easy to assess for text support: the less print, the easier it is to read. A picture book with one sentence per page requires less reading ability than a book with no pictures and 200 words per page. Print size can vary from 10 points to 18 points: happy to happy. A larger print size means fewer words, making a book easier to read.

The location of print can either support or hinder the reader. In the text samples provided in Figure 5, notice that the first has print in the same location on each page, while the second text has print in several different locations on each page. The second text requires greater reading competencies to understand the purpose of each section.

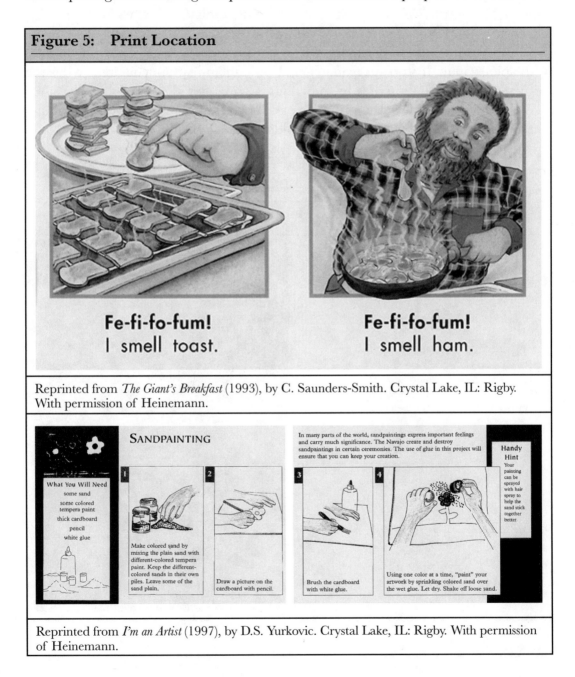

Figure 5:   Print Location

Fe-fi-fo-fum!
I smell toast.

Fe-fi-fo-fum!
I smell ham.

Reprinted from *The Giant's Breakfast* (1993), by C. Saunders-Smith. Crystal Lake, IL: Rigby. With permission of Heinemann.

Reprinted from *I'm an Artist* (1997), by D.S. Yurkovic. Crystal Lake, IL: Rigby. With permission of Heinemann.

Sometimes the way in which a text is divided among pages can make it more accessible, which supports readers with lesser reading competencies. An example of this supportive format is Longfellow's poem "Paul Revere's Ride" (Figure 6). Because the entire text has been divided among the pages and illustrated, the poem is accessible to third graders. In its traditional format of undivided text without pictures, the poem is more suitable for students at the middle school or high school level.

Other print conventions that provide text support for readers are punctuation and capitalization. If students read material with unfamiliar punctuation—a dash to designate an explanation of a term or, capitalizing every letter of a word—they may misunderstand the author's message and lose comprehension. Text containing unfamiliar print conventions can make reading more difficult.

Figure 6   Supportive Format for Difficult Text

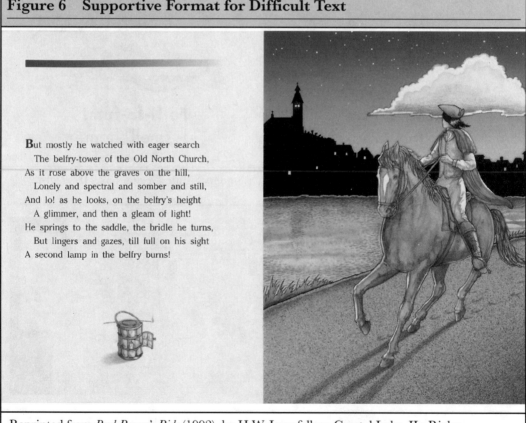

But mostly he watched with eager search
  The belfry-tower of the Old North Church,
As it rose above the graves on the hill,
  Lonely and spectral and somber and still,
And lo! as he looks, on the belfry's height
  A glimmer, and then a gleam of light!
He springs to the saddle, the bridle he turns,
  But lingers and gazes, till full on his sight
A second lamp in the belfry burns!

Reprinted from *Paul Revere's Ride* (1992), by H.W. Longfellow. Crystal Lake, IL: Rigby. With permission of Heinemann.

Language Structure

Language structure consists of the vocabulary, variance, and repetitiveness in sentence structure, rhyme and rhythm, and naturalness of language. Simple, familiar vocabulary is easy for readers to read and remember, while technical and multisyllabic words require more decoding skills. However, difficult vocabulary in a text where words are defined or explained in context assists readers in using advanced decoding skills with greater ease.

Simple sentences such as "I like dogs" require fewer reading competencies than a complex sentence such as "Due to the storm, the people in the town were without electricity and had to gather together to keep warm until the power was restored." The vocabulary used and the amount of interpretation required by readers are other factors that influence the simplicity or complexity of a sentence. A simple sentence like "Jump ship!" requires interpretation on the part of a reader to understand even though it is a two-word sentence.

Repetition, rhyme, and rhythm also affect the text support, and can make the reading less challenging. Books that repeat the same sentence page after page, changing only one word, are the most supportive (see Figure 7).

Lastly, the natural flow of language in text or in speech can make reading easier for beginning readers. In Figure 8 (see page 28), the first sample is typical of the language one might use, while the language in the second sample is more contrived, even though it uses simple vocabulary. The first sample is easily read by emergent readers, while the second requires more reading competencies.

Figure 7   Repetition

I found a shell.

I found a bucket.

Reprinted from *On the Beach* (1996), by C. Telford. Crystal Lake, IL: Rigby. With permission of Heinemann.

Figure 8   Natural Flow of Language

Reprinted from *Don't Leave Anything Behind!* (1993), by C. Krueger. Crystal Lake, IL: Rigby. With permission of Heinemann.

Reprinted from *Where Are the sunhats?* (1996), by B. Randell. Crystal Lake, IL: Rigby. With permission of Heinemann.

Language structure significantly influences the level of reading difficulty of a text. The greater the number of supportive structures, the easier the level of reading difficulty. Therefore, a text with repetitive sentences, simple vocabulary, and one line of print makes reading easier for a child with limited reading competencies.

Content

Content influences the level of reading difficulty because it requires familiarity or background knowledge of the subject in order for readers to comprehend. Nonfiction tends to be more difficult to read than fiction because one is reading to learn about someone or something. In fiction, the story line often carries the readers. Pictures and illustrations support text and may help to determine necessary reading competencies for readers. In beginning reading levels, the highest level of support is having text matched to a picture. For example, a picture of a boy eating an apple matched to text that reads "I am eating an apple" will be read more easily by children with limited reading competencies. Often, pictures accompany text and assist in comprehension but do not match text on a one-to-one basis. Finally, if the content requires readers to make significant interpretations as they read, then it will have a higher level of reading difficulty.

In leveling books, format, language structure, and content require simultaneous analysis to be effective. The criteria for each book level in a leveling system will define these areas, and the exemplar book for a level will demonstrate and reflect the criteria for that level.

Figure 9 (see page 30) demonstrates the following high levels of text difficulty in content, language structure, and format:

- nonfiction text discussing fantasy characters,
- variety of sentence structures including many complex sentences,
- concepts of text (Biblical stories, tribal stories, Greek mythology) requiring previous knowledge and experience in order to understand the text,
- text using parentheses to give examples and explanations, and
- sophisticated vocabulary.

Even though the article on giants is only two pages long, it requires the reading competencies of a beginning fourth grader to understand and be able to write a response that interprets the article. The article demonstrates how format, language structure, and content are analyzed together to determine text difficulty and matched to the appropriate reader.

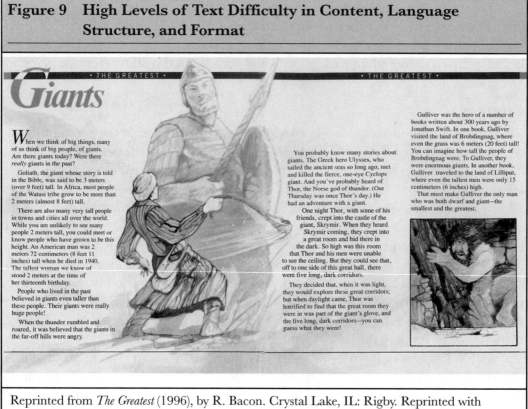

Leveling Steps

The leveling steps in this chapter explain the process for leveling books using any leveling system. The generic steps will become more specific once you have either selected or developed a leveling system. The leveling of books for primary and for intermediate grades are different in focus and substance. At the primary level, teachers focus on increasing the amount of text read at each level. At the intermediate level, the amount of text remains constant at one full page. In primary leveling, the text is closely analyzed for how much text support is available to assist the decoding process as the levels increase. In intermediate leveling, because students have already acquired decoding skills and strategies, the text is analyzed for the amount of text support available to aid comprehension. As a result of these differences, the steps to primary and intermediate leveling will be discussed separately.

Preparing Primary and Intermediate Level Books

The following steps prepare you to separate the primary books from the intermediate books and to assemble your required materials.

1. Separate the books into two groups, primary and intermediate, by using the criteria of amount of print, appropriateness for grade level, and vocabulary difficulty. Primary books will have one line to three fourths of a page of print throughout the book, simple vocabulary, and simple to moderately complex sentence structures. The topics should be appropriate for the age group as well. Intermediate books will have full pages of print, smaller print size, chapters, and a variety of moderate to complex sentence structures. The topics will stand out as more appropriate for this age group than for primary students. Some books can be deceptive as to the proper level, but you can correct any mistakes as you engage in the leveling process.

2. In front of each group of books, place a chart of the defined levels from the leveling system. Each chart will have the characteristics and instructional aspects for each level. If the leveling system does not provide a list or chart, you will have to develop one based on the exemplar book for each level. Use the areas of format, language structure, and content to analyze the exemplars.

3. Using exemplar books from each level of each group (primary and intermediate), open and spread them out in front of you. If the leveling system does not provide an exemplar book, you can use either the assessment book at that level or an already leveled book. Compare these books to the ones you are leveling in each group.

Decide whether to begin with primary or intermediate books and follow the steps appropriate to those books.

Steps for Leveling Primary Books (K to Mid-Grade 3)

Primary leveling focuses on fluency development and learning to read and therefore incorporates decoding skills, cueing strategies, vocabulary development, and phonics. The gradual increases in difficulty are dependent on the amount of text support provided: repetitive sentences, phrases, and words; rhyming and rhythm; match between text and pictures; simplistic language; and natural language or language similar to speech. The more the text displays these factors, the greater the support.

1. Divide the primary books into fiction, nonfiction, and poetry.

2. Divide the fiction books into three groups based solely on volume of print: (1) one or three lines per page, (2) one quarter to one third of a page of print, and (3) one full page of print. Many books will not be consistent in pages of print. Some may have mostly full pages with several half pages of print, so judge them by the amount of print on the majority of pages. The first print group will be for beginning levels of the system, the second group will be for middle levels, and the third group will be for the upper levels.

3. Divide the nonfiction books into print groups the same as in Step 2.

4. Using the fiction books and exemplar books from the leveling system, match up the text. Use the criteria charts or lists developed for the leveling system as a guideline.

5. Label the books with your selected code (color or number) and store them for use. As these newly leveled books are used you may note whether students read them easily or with difficulty. Re-evaluate your books after using them in instruction.

6. Using the nonfiction books and exemplar books from the leveling system, match the books to the appropriate exemplar level. Use the criteria charts or lists developed for the leveling system as a guideline. Because nonfiction text has a higher level of difficulty than fiction, do not hesitate to assign it to a higher level.

7. Label the nonfiction books with your selected code and store them for use. As you use these books, you will note that the students either read them easily or with difficulty. Re-evaluate your books based on their effectiveness during use in instruction.

8. Leveling poems is more involved because poems vary in length, vocabulary difficulty, and interpretation level. I recommend that individual poems be selected for instruction at the primary level and leveled based on the criteria for each level: vocabulary, sentence structure, and format.

9. Using the exemplar books and criteria charts of the leveling system, examine and analyze each poem for an appropriate level. Short poems with familiar vocabulary will be at the lower levels, and full-page poems with more sophisticated vocabulary will be at the higher levels.

10. Label the poems with your selected code for use in instruction.

As you level the primary books, you may find books that do not fit this level. Place these books in the intermediate group for leveling. Many picture books appear to be appropriate for primary levels, but the vocabulary and sentence structure make them too difficult. These books may be used at this level as read alouds, because the topics may not be interesting enough to intermediate children.

Steps for Leveling Intermediate Books (Mid-Grade 3 Through Grade 6)

The process for leveling books shifts somewhat at the Intermediate level. The focus in no longer on developing fluency but rather on increasing the ability to process and learn from text, including vocabulary development, interpretation skills, higher level thinking skills, and application and integration with various content subject areas. The distinguishing characteristics of a book's level lies with the organization, format, use of vocabulary, and text support to learn the content. Books that are easier to read will be a lower level than those books that are difficult to read or that require more interpretation on the part of the reader.

There are very few intermediate leveling systems that use subjective criteria. Most intermediate level books are leveled by using a readability formula: number of words per sentence, number of sentences, length of sentences, and number of syllables in a word. Chapter 4 discusses two leveling systems that use readability formulas and computer software to level intermediate books and generate lists of books for teachers. Using readability formulas and subjective criteria reduces the risk of presenting students a seemingly appropriate book but one they cannot read due to format, language structure, or content. Figures 10 (see page 34) and 11 (see page 35) illustrate this point. Using the Fry formula (Fry, Kress, & Fountoukidis, 1993), the text in Figure 10 is identified as a Grade 3 readability level, and the text in Figure 11 is identified as a Grade 7 readability level. If only this formula is used to level these books, we would see in instruction that these grade levels are inappropriate. Figure 10 is from a fiction text about an 11-year-old girl. The events and details in the book are inappropriate for a third grader, even though it is at a Grade 3 readability level. The mood, tone, and subtleties are more developmentally appropriate for Grades 5 or 6. The text in Figure 11 is identified as a Grade 7 readability level, yet the pages of print have pictures interspersed throughout the book that enhance comprehension. The text is more appropriate for 5th graders. Seventh graders might find this format somewhat immature.

Steps for Using a Readability Formula and Subjective Criteria

1. Divide the intermediate books into the grade-level groups of 3, 4, 5, and 6, using a readability formula such as Fry's (Fry, Kress, & Fountoukidis, 1993),

Figure 10 Grade 3 Readability Level

Now what? I turn around from washing the windshield and there's a big, brown dog with a gigantic pink tongue, and it's licking Corey's face.

"It's okay, Corey." I point to the dog's tail, which is wagging like a helicopter's rotor. "He wants to be friends." I put down my rag and bend down next to Corey. The dog tries to lick my face, and I notice a round tag on his collar.

"Howard," I read aloud. "32 Finch Street. Phone 555-4811. Well, Howard," I say to the dog, "this isn't 32 Finch Street. That's five blocks away. I think you're lost." Howard puts a dopey look on his face and wags his tail even harder.

"Tell you what," I say to him, "you stay here and mind Corey and I'll call your owner."

I go inside and try, but the phone is busy so I go back outside to check that I've got the right number. Howard's lying on his back with his legs in the air while Corey tickles his tummy, and I can't get anywhere near his collar to look. It will be quicker to walk him home at this rate.

"Dad, I'm walking a dog home. I'll only be half an hour," I call, as I find some rope.

"Have you finished the car?"

"Yeah."

"And put everything away?"

I tie Howard up to the drainpipe while I put away the hose and the buckets. Corey wanders inside. Just when I'm ready to go, our cat, Meatball, appears around the corner, sees Howard, and starts arching her back and spitting. Howard immediately goes into I-Hate-Cats mode, tries to get at Meatball, and strains wildly against the rope as Meatball dashes up the apple tree. The drainpipe gives a creak and starts to part company from the wall.

"Oh, no!" I quickly untie Howard, who's suddenly got the strength of a bull elephant, tie him around the base of the apple tree, and shove the drainpipe back against the wall. Unless you look closely you can't see that it's just sort of leaning there. Now I'm hoping that it doesn't rain for about five years – at least until I've made enough money to pay off all my other debts.

Reprinted from *Get a Grip, Pip!* (1995), by M. Clark. Crystal Lake, IL: Rigby. With permission of Heinemann.

Dale-Chall (Chall & Dale, 1995), or the Degrees of Reading Power (DRP-Booklink, 1999). (Sometimes publishers have lists divided by book readability.)

2. Divide the books into fiction, nonfiction, and poetry for each grade-level group. Within fiction and nonfiction, divide the books into genres.

3. Select the leveling system for the intermediate level, and spread before you the exemplar books for each level. Use the books and chart of criteria for the levels and follow the remaining procedures.

4. Using the genre list in Chapter 2, decide if the books within the nonfiction and fiction groups are appropriate for the grade level of instruction, reading assessment, or writing assessment. If the genre is appropriate, read the books to determine the difficulty level in terms of interpretation, vocabulary usage, language structure, format, organization, and content. Using the exemplar books from the leveling system, match the levels and label the books. If a genre is not appropriate for the grade level, label the book as a read aloud. However, because genre appropriateness is based partially on readability level, it will be unusual for a book to be in a grade level group and not be an appropriate genre. Keep in mind that nonfiction text tends to be more difficult to comprehend so when in doubt, raise the level.

5. Leveling poetry collections is more involved if the collections include a variety of types of poetry. In this case, use the leveling criteria with the more

Figure 11 Grade 7 Readability Level

In 1933, a new road was blasted out of the rock along the northern side of Loch Ness. Local newspapers reported many more monster sightings from this time on. Some people think that the blasting created underwater disturbances, causing the monster to surface from underground caves. Others believe that the road simply allowed more people a good view of the water – and anything that might appear in or on it!

STRANGE SPECTACLE ON LOCH NESS

Loch Ness has for generations been credited with being the home of a fearsome-looking monster, but, somehow or other, this legendary creature has always been regarded as a myth, if not a joke. Now, however, comes the news that the beast has been seen once more, for on Friday of last week, a well-known business man, who lives near Inverness, and his wife (a University graduate), when motoring along the north shore of the loch, were startled to see a tremendous upheaval on the loch, which previously had been as calm as the proverbial millpond. The lady was the first to notice the disturbance, and it was her sudden cries which drew her husband's attention to the water.

There, the creature rolled and plunged for fully a minute, its body resembling that of a whale, and the water cascading and churning like a simmering caldron.

Soon, however, it disappeared in a boiling mass of foam. Both onlookers confessed that there was something uncanny about the whole thing, because, apart from its enormous size, the beast, in taking the final plunge, sent out waves that were big enough to have been caused by a passing steamer. The watchers waited for half an hour in the hope that the monster (if such it was) would come to the surface again; but they had seen the last of it.

The Courier, May 2, 1933

Reprinted from *The Loch Ness Monster Mystery* (1995), by M. Fleming and V. King. Crystal Lake, IL: Rigby. With permission of Heinemann.

complex poetry so students will be successful with the poems. If the collection has similar types of poems, then match the entire collection to the exemplars and level criteria.

These steps will guide you through the process of leveling books for the process-approach or literature-based program. As a trial for leveling books, select some titles from a system's leveled list of books without checking the level. Follow the leveling guidelines and see how close you come to the system's level. Because of the subjectivity within leveling systems try to come within one level. It is better to level conservatively at first or place books at a higher level and re-level lower if the student finds the text easier to read at that level. Using the books in instruction is the ultimate test of how well you matched the level to the reader. The reader should always experience success with the initial reading of a text, which keeps motivation high.

Chapter 4

Comparisons of Leveling Systems

> Gradients of difficulty are essential for teachers making good decisions about materials they select for children to read, but all gradients are inevitably fallible.
>
> (Clay, 1991, p. 201)

Clay's statement explains the controversy about which leveling system is most appropriate. No one leveling system is completely successful with all students. Therefore, in your selection of a leveling system, consider these aspects. How flexible is the system in meeting various students' needs? Does the system have enough materials already leveled in order to get started? What is the system's instructional focus or framework?

In this chapter, a few systems currently used in classrooms will be compared and contrasted. Because the selection criteria for some systems are unclear or not specific, I have made interpretations or stated that they are not available. Compared were the areas of instructional focus, assessing the level of a student and when to move a student, accessibility of leveled materials, and advantages and disadvantages. The brief comparisons will provide the means to investigate an appropriate leveling system.

The Lexile Framework and the Degrees of Reading Power

These two systems are closely related to traditional readability formulas and use highly researched and sophisticated formulas. Both systems use computer-generated levels (see Figures 12 and 13 on page 38). Teachers using these systems will have to compare the levels to familiar books until the new terminology is learned. For example, *Frog and Toad Are Friends* (Lobel, 1970), which is leveled at the 400 Lexile, second-grade level, can be used for instruction with students who are functioning at that lev-

Figure 12: The Lexile Framework

Instructional Focus	Assessment	Teacher Accessibility	Disadvantages	Advantages
Reading Comprehension Grades 1–12.	Uses standardized tests.	Levels are computer generated and available.	Lowest level of 200 does not reach low enough for beginning first graders. No guides about how to instruct per level. No criteria or explanation for the difference in levels (i.e., How is 345 different from 360?).	Levels go to upper elementary and beyond. Levels are consistent due to use of formula.

Source: *The Lexile Framework*. (1996). Durham, NC: Meta Metrics, Inc.

Figure 13: The Degrees of Reading Power

Instructional Focus	Assessment	Teacher Accessibility	Disadvantages	Advantages
Reading Comprehension Grades 1–12.	Uses Degrees of Reading Power Test.	Levels are computer generated and available.	Lowest level of 27 DRP is not low enough for beginning first graders. No guides about how to instruct per level. No criteria or explanation for the difference in levels. (i.e., How is 45 DRP different from 52 DRP?)	Levels go to upper elementary and beyond. Levels are consistent due to use of formula. Provides literature and textbook leveling.

Source: *DRP-Booklink*. (1999). Brewster, NY: Touchstone Applied Science Associates.

el. Standardized tests are used to determine the appropriate levels of students. The Lexile Framework uses the Stanford Achievement Test, and the Degrees of Reading Power (DRP) uses its own standardized measure, the Degrees of Reading Power Test.

The biggest disadvantage of these two systems seems to be that the formulas deal with text in isolation from the format, quantity, or organization of the language. For example, in the DRP system, the book *Mooncake* (Asch, 1983) is leveled at 46 DRP, which is similar to *Superfudge* (Blume, 1980) at 45 DRP. *Superfudge* is a 166-page chapter book while *Mooncake* is a 28-page picture book, so different reading competencies are required for each book although there is only a 1-point difference between the books. However, if you analyze only books of the same format (i.e., all chapter books), the formulas work quite well for establishing text-level difficulty.

The Primary Readability Index

This leveling system (Gunning, 1998) uses some aspects of a readability formula and other more subjective criteria such as format of the book (i.e., one picture and one sentence per page). Using both formula and subjective criteria, Gunning developed an assessment that provides not only the exemplars of the levels, but also the means to determine at which level a student is reading (see Figure 14). This system was validated with data from the reading clinic where Gunning works.

Figure 14: The Primary Readability Index

Instructional Focus	Assessment	Teacher Accessibility	Disadvantages	Advantages
Oral fluency predominant, with some comprehension.	Primary Readability Index Inventory.	About 1000 books listed in text, with specific procedures for leveling included in text.	Limited to primary grades (K–2). Leveling procedure is time consuming. Mostly fiction. No guides for instruction at levels.	Objective factors make leveling more consistent than using subjective factors only. Data supports consistency of levels. Assessment matches the leveling criteria.

Source: Gunning, T.G. (1998). *Best Books for Beginning Readers*. Boston: Allyn & Bacon.

Figure 15: The Shoebox Library

Instructional Focus	Assessment	Teacher Accessibility	Disadvantages	Advantages
Predominantly reading fluency.	Behavior checklist for each level.	8 books per level with additional books listed for use in instruction.	No specific book or standard expectations for assessment. Criteria for levels is broad and general. No specific guidelines for leveling own books. Few books at a level. Limited to grades 1–2. Text difficulty range of books within a level seems quite broad.	Specific instructional activities for each book. Can be purchased from one publisher.

Source: Pinnell, G.S. (1996). *Teacher's Guide Shoebox Library*. New York: Scholastic.

The Shoebox Library

This leveling system is a curriculum supplement to the *Literacy Place* (1996) basal series and is intended for use in the instruction of guided reading or small-group reading instruction (see Figure 15). In the *Teacher's Guide* (Pinnell, 1996), the levels are explained. The guide also includes specific phonics, comprehension, and writing activities for each book. The assessment involves the observation of behaviors as students read. Details of the behaviors for each level are outlined in a check-off chart.

Reading Recovery

The levels for this system were developed by Marie Clay for Reading Recovery, a first-grade intervention program that involves one-to-one tutoring 30 minutes per

Figure 16: Reading Recovery

Instructional Focus	Assessment	Teacher Accessibility	Disadvantages	Advantages
Development of oral fluency in first graders.	Reading Recovery tests include running records, concepts about print test, writing test, vocabulary test, dictation test, and sounds and letters test.	Extensive teacher training in RR is necessary before system can be used. After training and use of the program, teacher can begin leveling books. Many leveled book lists are available to the trained Reading Recovery teachers.	Requires extensive teacher training. Limited to first-grade students. Level criteria is mostly subjective.	Highly successful program with first graders. Consistent instruction and assessment using the leveled books. Training is beneficial to instruction for all students. Text difficulty between levels is minimal so students feel successful and therefore progress through the levels more quickly.

Source: Based on information supplied by Reading Recovery teachers.

day (see Figure 16). The program requires extensive training, usually 1 year of study, and subsequent periodic training throughout a teacher's career. The success rate of this intervention program is high and well documented. The assessments for this program are specific and most are included in *The Early Detection of Reading Difficulties: A Diagnostic Survey With Recovery Procedures* (Clay, 1985).

Because the sources are not readily available to teachers who are not in the Reading Recovery program, I have made interpretations that explain the specific characteristics for each level.

The differences among the levels appear to be based on understandings about print, natural language versus book text, supportive text, and high frequency vocabulary. In the first levels (Levels 1 and 2), students learn where print is located and are directed by the teacher to repeat the repetitive text. They also learn to use

Chapter 5

The Weaver Reading/Writing Stages

> After 30 years of teaching reading, it is still so rewarding to see children partici-
> pate in reading as an adventure rather than a chore. Brenda Weaver's insightful process
> has made that adventure a reality for so many more youngsters. Her leveling of chil-
> dren's literature or trade books has set a framework for a developing reader to read with
> success. Her frame for leveling books has greatly helped my students to become em-
> powered readers.
>
> (Ann Mele, reading teacher, Sachem Public Schools, Long Island, New York)

Leveling books is a means to enable a child to be successful in literacy development. The Weaver Reading/Writing Stages were developed to enable all students
to be successful and competent communicators. This program, which has been
used for 12 years in the Skaneateles in upstate New York and replicated by schools
nationally and internationally, began with a trip to New Zealand in 1988 on a state
scholarship to study the country's language arts program. Upon my return, the
process of creating a rich, literate experience for our children began. The New
Zealand program was analyzed and revised to fit a structure with which U.S. teachers could relate and incorporate into their knowledge of literacy. An implementation
plan was developed, staff development workshops arranged, and experts in the literacy field were called on to work with the teachers and myself as we progressed.
As part of the implementation plan, a yearly evaluation was conducted to reflect on
and revise elements of the program as necessary.

The Weaver Reading/Writing Stages includes six teaching components, the
K–6 leveling system, assessments based on the stages, hundreds of literature titles, integration with other subject areas, and continuous staff development. This program is different from many in that it does not rely on specific textbooks or a published reading program, but rather on teacher knowledge, understanding, and skill in
literacy development.

The Six Components

In the program, teachers provide instruction using six components to ensure a balanced literacy program. Instruction is provided equally among the following components: *reading aloud, shared reading, guided writing, guided reading, independent reading,* and *independent writing. Reading aloud* to children gives them experiences with text beyond their present ability and introduces them to books they might not read on their own. It also develops listening skills and comprehension. *Shared reading* and *guided writing* are the two components in which teachers deliver the grade-level literacy curriculum to all students.

A grade-level scope and sequence have been developed that outline the skills, strategies, and suggested texts for each quarter of the school year. At the end of each quarter, the students take a reading and writing assessment that reflects the skills, strategies, and concepts of the scope and sequence. Although shared reading and guided writing consist primarily of whole-group instruction, there is often small-group instruction as well. Examples of scope and sequence for Grade 1 and Grade 5 follow:

Example 3: Grade 1 Literacy Focus Areas

Necessary Elements/Strategies for 1.1

Shared Reading

> Uses initial and final sounds when reading.
>
> Rhymes words by changing and writing initial sounds.
>
> Puts separate sounds together orally to form words.
>
> Distinguishes sound differences in words auditorially.
>
> Recognizes differences and similarities between words.
>
> Understands that a story has a beginning, middle, and end.
>
> Completes a cloze exercise orally.
>
> Recognizes exclamation point and explains purpose.
>
> Answers detail questions orally about story in complete sentences.
>
> Recognizes differences between illustrators.
>
> Understands the literary patterns: familiar cultural sequence (review alphabet, numbers) of colors, days, months; and repetitive guided writing.
>
> Writes a sentence with noun and verb.

Uses capital letters at beginning of sentences and punctuation at end.

Writes simple dictated sentences. Examples: I like dogs. The boy is tall. The ball is big. Jack likes to play. Sue likes to run. I like cake. Cake is good to eat. Are you going home? Where is Jack? I want to go with you.

Independently writes own simple rewrite: I like _____.

Tells orally beginning, middle, and end of own story, but writes only a sentence or two.

Rewrites in a group the literary patterns: familiar cultural sequence (review alphabet, numbers) of colors, days, months; and repetitive.

Review and/or Expansion Elements/Strategies for 1.1

Shared Reading

Understands the direction of reading (left to right and return).

Understands ending punctuation of period, question mark.

Recognizes initial and final consonant sounds.

Understands word boundaries in print.

Uses voice-print match effectively.

Understands sequence of a story.

Segments words and syllables in story.

Guided Writing

Draws a picture to convey a message.

Reviews printing of upper and lower case letters.

Uses writing of words to convey message.

Example 4: Grade 5 Literacy Assessment Guide

Reading Skills/Strategies for Instruction for 5.1
Key: LB = *The Language Book* (1991)   WS = *Write Source 2000* (1995)

Defines narration and exposition (WS, 127).

Differentiates between narrative/expository text (WS, 078).

Identifies and discusses story elements (WS, 387).

Identifies and discusses point of view (LB, 187; WS, 387).

Utilizes skimming and scanning (LB, 205–206).

Utilizes paraphrasing (LB, 210).

Writing Skills/Strategies for Instruction

Understands expository writing (LB, 169–170, 225).

Understands narrative writing (LB, 123, 165–166, 185–190, 227).

Understands characteristics of different genre (see end papers of *The Language Book*).

Writes to meet both the specific form and topic.

Understands report writing process (LB, 202-204).

Understands story writing (LB, 123–124, 185–190).

Listening Skills/Strategies for Instruction

Understands the tips for listening (LB, 122, WS 402–404).

Understands the process of note taking (LB, 207–209; WS, 413–417).

Prepares graphic organizers to remember details.

Responds to questions appropriately and completely.

Guided reading consists of small-group instruction in reading and response writing based on reading ability, skill need, or book title. In the primary grades, these groups are based on reading ability. Once the class is divided into small groups, the students will remain there for approximately one month, but the grouping is flexible and can be changed when necessary. The small guided-reading groups provide students with the appropriate level of instruction in reading and writing that is vital to successful literacy development.

The components of *independent reading* and *independent writing* involve students in their own personal reading and writing through self-selection of books. These two components are usually carried out during the guided reading time. In independent reading, students select books to read from the library or a book box. In independent writing, students maintain a personal writing folder that contains personal writing topics, drafts, and finished writing. Students can sometimes select partners to collaborate with on writing a story or play. These independent writing pieces are shared with the entire class in a group sharing session or class meeting.

All components utilize leveled books in different ways. The read-aloud books are above students' reading levels, the shared reading books are at the level of the majority of students in the class, and the guided reading books are at the instructional level of individual students. The independent reading books are at the easiest level for reading by the students and do not require teacher assistance to read.

write stories. At the intermediate grades, the students study genres in depth and are assessed on these genres. The students are required to read silently a selection in a specific genre and respond to higher level comprehension questions. They are also asked to write in various genres. The assessments are reviewed and revised periodically to ensure that expectations and standards remain high.

Materials

The materials used in the program are predominantly literature books and trade books. The materials are selected by the teachers who meet periodically to suggest titles and review books. The books are leveled using the Weaver leveling system and placed on a reference list for a specific grade level. Each grade list has titles matching the content and the Weaver level appropriate for instruction at that grade level. The materials are stored in a common bookroom in the school.

Integration

A key element of the program is authentic literacy tasks or reading real-life books for real purposes. Naturally, teachers select and use books that further the subject areas they teach. Using real books instead of textbooks to teach the Revolutionary War or animal habitat promotes high motivation and develops students who are avid readers of all types of books. Teachers can easily teach the various viewpoints on a historical event or the most recent study of animal behavior when they use real books. Students often will bring books from home on the subject being taught in school. The students understand how reading and writing are life-long endeavors.

Staff Development

A very important factor in the program is the staff development of teachers. Teachers are taught to be experts in literacy development and receive a great deal of support from me, the language arts coordinator, and from other support staff such as the reading and special education teachers. All new teachers receive this same high level of staff development and support.

The Results

After years of working with teachers and students using this program, I have found that it provides for the needs of all students, and its success is supported by standardized test data. The New York State Education Department rates our school district as an "average needs district" on its three category levels of high need, average need, and low need. The standardized test data indicate that over 90% of students are average or above in reading ability. On the new performance-based assessments of New York State in Grade 4, 91% of students scored above the minimum standard. This was the top score achieved in all school districts (student population over 50) in New York State. Over the years, these scores have continued to reach these levels in spite of the increase in at-risk students entering the schools. I believe these high scores are a result of our unique literacy program.

However, high achievement test scores are not the only indicator of a high literacy rate in this school district. These students love to read and write, often choosing to read or write instead of playing ball on the playground. The library circulation rates have doubled every year since the program was implemented. Parents remark in amazement that their children choose to read and write as a home activity. This enthusiasm for literacy is a cherished result of our literacy program.

The Weaver Reading/Writing Stages are a collaborative effort on the part of myself and the teachers. The stages work well and are highly successful in developing effective communicators.

Chapter 6

Where Do I Go From Here?

We were one district with four elementary schools, each with a different yet ineffective reading program that met few of the students' needs. I was given the responsibility to implement one program that would meet the district's newly developed reading philosophy, while addressing the needs of ESL, special education, gifted, as well as the average student. Brenda Weaver, working with our district, helped us to achieve a dramatic turnaround within two years. We began with the leveling of our books and then assessing and placing each student at their appropriate level. Staff development training sessions helped teachers to understand the process and program, and to implement it in their classrooms. We have not only changed how our teachers teach, but changed forever how our students learn to read. The results of all this work were immediate and dramatic when last January our students scored extremely high on our state's new fourth-grade English/Language Arts assessment.

(Dr. Deanne J. Gerstel, Assistant to the Superintendent, Mineola Public Schools, Long Island, New York)

From the viewpoint expressed in the letter, moving in the direction of using leveled books is a journey and a challenge, but the rewards are great. Children become life-long readers and writers, and that is what literacy education is about. The following are additional suggestions for moving students toward successful literacy learning.

Begin Where You Are

To begin, assess where you are by answering these questions:

How much do I know about the process approach to literacy?

What type of reading program do I have? What do I need to revise in order to use it in the process approach? What literature is used in the language arts program?

What facilities do I have for storing books and materials?

What techniques do I use to teach reading and writing?

To determine where you want to go, answer these questions:

Do I want to use leveled books exclusively?

Do I want to use the readers and books already in a program and supplement them with leveled books?

Do I want to incorporate the techniques of a program in the process approach?

I recommend writing out your goals for this process and revising them as you go. Changing to a leveled system is not a quick process, but it is worthwhile.

Learning About Process Literacy

When you know where you are and where you want to go, you want to learn the aspects of literacy that are unfamiliar to you. Process literacy is defined as the approach to reading and writing that involves instruction in strategies and skills, the role of the teacher as a facilitator of learning, the development of support structures in learning, and the students as active learners. Reading Recovery is an example of process literacy. Process literacy is based on the most recent understanding of how children acquire literacy. Many books are available about this approach and its aspects. Read these resources, attend courses and staff development workshops, or contact consultants to acquire additional knowledge and understanding.

Action Plans

Action plans consist of goals, activities to achieve goals, and evaluation of the activities. They are critical to the successful implementation of any program and are documented evidence that the implementation is working or needs revision.

In developing action plans, evaluation is the key element. You will want to be sure that the evaluation method used is appropriate for assessing or measuring goal achievement. For example, a goal might be that students read more books. An inappropriate evaluation method would be to establish silent reading time in the classroom. Although this activity would encourage reading, it will not adequately document the number of books being read. An appropriate evaluation method is to document school library circulation.

Developing and documenting action plans demonstrates commitment to goals, which leads to success.

The first step is developing a literacy program using leveled books. As educators, we are committed to finding more effective ways of teaching literacy. It is a journey that must begin with a first step. We owe this to our students.

Glossary

Assessment: an evaluation of learned competencies.

Comprehension patterns: written organization of text usually written in one of six different patterns to convey a message: chronological, comparison, description, concept by example, problem/resolution, and cause/effect.

Content: the subject or topic of text material.

Exemplar Book: a book that accurately depicts the criteria for a specific book level in a leveling system.

Format: the style or way in which type is set, how pictures are displayed, the print size, and paragraph length. Books with small print, long paragraphs, and few pictures are more difficult to read than those with larger print, shorter paragraphs, and many pictures.

Framework: the structure or scope and sequence of a literacy program

Grade level appropriateness: material that fits the achievement level and interests of students at a specific grade level.

Instruction: the teaching skills, strategies, and content in a literacy program.

Interpretation: how a reader uses previous experience and knowledge to understand a text.

Language structure: the complexity of sentences and use of vocabulary within a text.

Leveling: selecting books to match the competencies of a reader or writer.

Leveling system: a structure that determines how books are sequenced and used in a literacy program.

Organization: the arrangement of text in terms of comprehension patterns and sentence placement within a text. For example, is there a chronological sequence used in the text, or is it a listing of facts?

Readability: the level of difficulty of text at which a student can read.

Subject appropriateness: a topic appropriate to the age level of students. For example, a book about taking a teddy bear to bed would be appropriate for kindergarten or first-grade children, ages 5–6.

Text support: the degree to which format, language structure, and content influence the difficulty of reading written text; a high level of text support means that the written text is easy or requires less sophisticated reading competencies to read the text.

Vocabulary usage: words in a text that are used and understood by students at a specific grade level. Also, words that help readers understand the vocabulary by defining it or using other words to explain it.

References

Brandt, R.S. (1998). *Powerful learning*. Alexandria, VA: Association for Supervision and Curriculum Development.

Brandt, R.S. (1988). Conclusion: Conceptions of content. In R.S. Brandt (Ed.), *Content of the curriculum* (pp. 187–197). Alexandria, VA: Association for Supervision and Curriculum Development.

Chall, J.S., & Dale, E. (1995). *Readability revisited: The new Dale-Chall readability formula*. Cambridge, MA: Brookline.

Clay, M.M. (1979). *Reading: The patterning of complex behavior*. Portsmouth, NH: Heinemann.

Clay, M.M. (1985). The early detection of reading difficulties: A diagnostic survey with recovery procedures (3rd ed.). Portsmouth, NH: Heinemann.

Clay, M.M. (1991). *Becoming literate: The construction of inner control*. Portsmouth, NH: Heinemann.

Cooper, J.D. (1993). *Literacy: Helping children construct meaning*. Boston: Houghton Mifflin.

English, F.W. (1986). Who is in charge of the curriculum? In H.J. Walberg & J.W. Keefe (Eds.), *Rethinking reform: The principal's dilemma* (pp. 25–30). Reston, VA: National Association of Secondary School Principals.

Fountas, I.C., & Pinnell, G.S. (1996). *Guided reading: Good first teaching for all children*. Portsmouth, NH: Heinemann.

Fountas, I.C., & Pinnell, G.S. (1999). *Matching books to readers: Using leveled books in guided reading, K–3*. Portsmouth, NH: Heinemann.

Fry, E.B., Kress, J.E., & Fountoukidis, D.L. (1993). *The reading teacher's book of lists*. New York: Prentice-Hall.

Fullan, M.G. (1991). *The new meaning of educational change*. New York: Teachers College Press.

Gunning, T.G. (1998). Best books for beginning readers. Boston: Allyn & Bacon.

Meta Metrics. (1996). *The Lexile Framework*. Durham, NC: Author.

Mooney, M. (1988). *Developing life-long readers*. Wellington, New Zealand: Department of Education.

Nolan, J., & Francis, P. (1992). Changing perspectives in curriculum and instruction. In C. Glickman (Ed.), *Supervision in transition*. Alexandria, VA: Association for Supervision and Curriculum Development.

Pinnell, G.S. (1996). *Teacher's guide shoebox library*. New York: Scholastic.

Presseisen, B.Z. (1988). Avoiding the battle at Curriculum Gulch: Teaching thinking and content. *Educational Leadership, 45*(70), 7–8.

Routman, R. (1988). *Transitions: From literature to literacy*. Portsmouth, NH: Heinemann.

Scholastic. (1996). *Literacy place*. New York: Author.

Sebranek, V., Meyer, V., & Kemper, D. (1995). *Write source 2000*. Wilmington, MA: Great Source Education.

Touchstone Applied Science Associates. (1999). *DRP-Booklink*. Brewster, NY: Author.

Vygotsky, L.S. (1978). *Mind in society. The development of higher psychological processes*. (M. Cole, V. John-Steiner, S. Scribner, & E. Souberman, Eds. and Trans.). Cambridge, MA: Harvard University Press. (Original work published 1934)

Children's Book References

Asch, F. (1983). *Mooncake*. New York: Simon & Schuster.

Blume, J. (1980). *Superfudge*. New York: Dell.

Kehoe, C. (1989). *Green footprints*. Crystal Lake, IL: Rigby.

Lobel, A. (1970). *Frog and toad are friends*. New York: HarperCollins.

Paterson, K. (1977). *The bridge to Terabithia*. New York: Harper Trophy.

Randell, B. (1997). *The busy beavers*. Crystal Lake, IL: Rigby.

Reeder, P. (1997). *Animals*. Bothell, WA: The Wright Group.

Rylant, C. (1996). Henry and Mudge series. New York: Simon & Schuster.

White, E.B. (1952). *Charlotte's web*. New York: Scholastic.

Index

Page references followed by *f* indicate figures.